You Can Make It

on

BROKEN PIECES

God Bless you forever...
Enjoy the "Gift of Life"
On Purpose

2012

You Can Make It
on
BROKEN PIECES

Delores R. Garvin, PhD

Kingdom Living Publishing
Fort Washington, MD

Cover design by TLH Designs, Chicago, IL
www.tlhdesigns.com

Published by
Kingdom Living Publishing
10905 Livingston Road
Fort Washington, MD 20744
www.kingdomlivingbooks.com

ISBN 978-0-9799798-5-9

Printed in the United States of America.

Presented To

Mother W. Rinehart

From

Dr. Delores R. Barwin

Date

_9-22-12_

But they that wait upon the LORD shall renew their
strength; they shall mount up with wings as eagles;
they shall run, and not be weary; and they shall walk,
and not faint (Isaiah 40:31).

Dedication

I dedicate this book

To my family: husband Abraham, daughters Adria and Khristahl, her husband Keith and their daughters Keirrah and Kennedi, grandparents' sweethearts. Thank you for your love and support.

To my sister Betty, who continues to encourage me by saying, "You can do it!"

To my brother Joe and his wife Minnie for their spiritual guidance.

To my brother Tommy and his wife Paulette, who continue to encourage and support me.

I pray this book will inspire us all as we grow in grace.

Acknowledgments

To God, the Creator of all things; Jesus Christ, Lord and Savior; the presence of the Holy Spirit.

To my parents Isaac and Annie Bell Randolph (deceased), my Sister Hannah (deceased); my Brother Willie Isaac (deceased) and his wife Lula; and Brother Willie James (deceased) and his wife Blondell.

To my awesome Spiritual Leaders who have empowered me to walk in the will of God always:

Apostle Nehemiah Rhinehart, Sr., DHL
& Dr. Wilhelmina Rhinehart

Bishop Joe L. Randolph, Th.D
& Dr. Minnie L. Randolph

Rev. Dr. Hallie Lawson Reeves, ACPE Supervisor

To Apostle Anthony T. Mays who encouraged me to write this book several years ago.

To all of my sisters and brothers in Christ who continues to encourage, support, and love me.

To members and friends of "New Life Praise Community, Inc."

To my friend and colleague Chaplain Annie Blackwell.

I express my gratitude for Irma McKnight's expertise and time in polishing my manuscript, directing, and assisting me on this project.

Table of Contents

Foreword

In her book, *"You Can Make It on Broken Pieces,"* Dr. Delores Garvin endeavors to help her readers understand that our whole life revolves around our "Story." Our "Story" begins with our first breath and ends with our last breath. Then comes our final hour, when once again our "Story" is repeated.

In her many courses in Clinical Pastoral Education, Dr. Garvin learned how to translate her patient parishioners' stories into feelings. She further learned how to explore those feelings, which her patient parishioners had bottled up inside themselves for such a long time. By exploring the darkness, the confusion, and the pain, she learned that her patient parishioners touched on the pain; and by touching the pain, the patient found a measure of healing.

Dr. Garvin makes it clear in her book that darkness and light need not oppose each other, but can and often complement each other. Without the brokenness in our lives, the joy of finding wholeness would not be complete.

The telling of one's own story requires courage. Very often we want to lift up that which appears impressive to others; nevertheless, Dr. Garvin has made use of her whole story—the good, the bad, and the ugly. She has also made use of her "I can do all things through Christ who strengthens me" power. This "I can" power is the vehicle which opens her up to her creation, and this "I can" power continues to propel her toward success.

Congratulations Dr. Garvin.... I am glad to know you....

The Reverend Hallie Lawson Reeves,
M.DIV., L.H.D.
(APC) BCC, (UMC) BCC, ACPE Supervisor

Introduction

The purpose of this book is to help others see that they can take stumbling blocks and use them as pieces to move them to higher levels in their journey. Get excited about your life. God has given each one of us a measure of grace—free. We have many choices in life, choices to be joyful, or choices to be sad. Make preparations to be joyful every day. If for some reasons you missed your golden opportunity, do not let your past dictate your future. Start making changes today. With God all things are possible.

⁴²And the soldiers' counsel was to kill the prisoners, lest any of them should swim out, and escape. ⁴³But the centurion, willing to save Paul, kept them from their purpose; and commanded that they which could swim should cast themselves first into the sea, and get to land: ⁴⁴And the rest, some on boards, and some on broken pieces of the ship. And so it came to pass, that they escaped all safe to land (Acts 27:42-44).

This is a story about Apostle Paul who was a prisoner on a ship. When I read this Scripture, I think about the hostage situations and the storms in my life. As demonstrated in this Scripture, God's presence was with the prisoners. When they thought all hope was gone, God used His vessel, Apostle Paul, to let them know they could make it on broken pieces. God has been forever present in my life and He has used many vessels to grant me broken pieces so I could endure the storms in my life.

In the twenty-seventh chapter of Acts, it was evident that God was on the ship, as God is forever present in our lives. We will always be faced with challenges. When we overcome one challenge, we will be handed a new challenge. Some of these challenges could be difficult or overwhelming, especially when there is no system in place. We have a built in system with God. We must trust in God and recognize and embrace His presence. God will reveal Himself to us. On the ship, Paul advised them not to go forward, but the man in charge refused to listen to him. The storm put everyone's life in danger, the centurion, soldiers, prisoners, and the owners.

When I look back over my life, I can see the hand of God everywhere. God protected me even when I did not know I needed protection. For each step that I took, God was forever present. For each broken piece that I used to move to the next level, I became stronger. There is power, God's power, in each piece.

I pray that by sharing the challenges that I endured in my life you will find hope in God when you are going through a storm in your life.

Chapter 1

Born into Brokenness

I grew up on a farm in the rural area of Calhoun County in South Carolina. I was the last child born to my parents. They already had six children when I was born. They had other children, but they died before I was born. One child died at three years and I think two others died at birth. During my entire life, there were seven children.

My oldest siblings had moved away from home by the time I was old enough to know them. The oldest sister was fifteen years my senior. Two brothers were right behind her in age, approximately two years apart. They left home when I was very young, so my first recollection of them was when they came home to visit. During my formative years, I lived in the house with my parents and three siblings. My father was a sharecropper. He harvested cotton for as far back as I can remember. He worked for a white family who were farmers and they allowed him to live on their farm in a small four-room house. It had a living room, kitchen, one bedroom for my parents, next to the living room, and one bedroom for me and my three siblings, next to the kitchen. The children's bedroom was the largest, with a full bed on each side of the room. The girls slept together in one bed and the boys slept together in the other bed.

Our bathroom, called an outhouse, was located in the back of the house. The trip to the bathroom at night was scary; we never knew what would be lurking outside late at night. We did not worry too much in the winter time because it was very cold outside and people or animals were not moving around too much, but in the summer time we had to look out for snakes, which were plentiful in our neck of the woods. There was no central heating in the house; we had a stove in the kitchen, where many delicious meals were prepared, and a fireplace in the living room. The stove and the fireplace kept the house warm as long as we continued to add wood to them. Keeping wood in the house and on the front porch was one of the many responsibilities for my siblings and me. During the night when all of the wood burned out, it got really cold. We slept under quilts and blankets to keep warm. One person — usually one of my brothers — would get up and start the fire in the morning to warm up the house before everyone else got up. My father did not get up unless he had been on one of his all night drinking binges. Then he would burn all of the wood and make us go outside and cut more and bring it into the house during the night. It did not matter which child he called on; that depended on his mood, and who he felt like punishing at that time.

We got our water from a pump that was also outside in an area close to the fields. I was told the water was coming from a spring underneath the ground. We used this water for drinking and washing. My grandparents, who lived in another part of the county, had a "well" in their yard, which was their only source of water. I was told the outside pump was an upgrade. Ironically, my mother would boil the water to wash clothes, but we drank the water directly from the pump. I think something was wrong with that picture. I get it that she wanted to sterilize the clothes, but in retrospect, I think we should have been sterilizing the drinking water as well. As a matter of fact, the drinking water should have taken precedent over the clothes. Anyway, we lived through it all.

While my father worked for the white family doing their farm work, he used his family to harvest his share, which was cotton. He was renting a field where he used to plant his cotton. The cotton-picking season came around the same time that our school year started. My sister and I stayed home and picked cotton for the first three days of the week before we could go to school. The eldest brother played on the football team, so therefore he had to go to school every day, and the other brother drove the school bus, so he had to go to school every day.

Not being able to go to school was very disheartening for my sister and me. When all the other children were preparing for school, we were preparing to go to the cotton field. We prayed everyday for it to rain so we could go to school. I remembered one of those rain days I went to school on Monday and my teacher gave me a speaking part in a play that would commence on Friday. I was so happy about my assignment. I studied my part all week and recited it to my family every chance I got. I did not go back to school until Friday because we had to make up that rain day. When I got to school on Friday, the teacher had given the part to another student who happened to be the smartest student in the class. My heart was broken because I was very proud to have the part in the play and I was well prepared. I remember wearing a magenta jumper with a white blouse under it. I was looking extra spiffy that day. I never forgot that incident or the pain, but I did not let that incident deter me from my studies. I studied very hard so I could keep my grades up.

I do not remember how long we worked under those conditions, but my sister and I never missed a grade. We always passed to the next class with good grades. It was God's strength that kept us in the right frame of mind. I was broken, but determined to excel in school. At the time, I did not know the importance of an education, but my father and my mother stressed it.

My father was also an entrepreneur and an avid hunter. He had a little operation going on down in the woods where he only went at nighttime. None of us were allowed to go to his nightspot, but every once in a while he would bring something home in a mason jar that looked like lemonade but tasted really sour. (I think it was supposed to be corn liquor; but it wasn't completely processed). I could always tell when he drank some of his concoction, because his mood would change immediately. He became talkative and sometimes his behavior would become aggressive.

In the area of South Carolina where we lived, the farmers hunted for game such as rabbits, squirrels, opossum, raccoon, and deer. For each animal, there was a specific season for hunting. I remember my father hunting a few times, but I do not remember him bringing any game home. He did not have a hunting partner so he always took one of his children with him. I cannot remember him taking the boys with him, but he took my sister and me with him one night and left us by the fence while he went further into the woods. It was so dark until we could not see anything around us; we could not see each other or my father. We heard him coming back because he was talking to himself, but he did not bring anything with him. That was the first and the last time I remember him hunting. In retrospect, I do not think he was hunting that night. I think he went to the neighbor's house to buy some corn liquor and he probably wanted some company. Corn liquor, even though it was illegal to sell or make, was very popular during that time. Many people made the liquor in the woods and sold it from their homes. I think my father was trying to get into that market, but he was not very successful.

My mother was a domestic worker. She worked for the same family for which my father worked. She cleaned houses for the parents, their three sons, and their families. After she finished her work, she came home and cooked dinner, cleaned house, and worked in the field with us. She never complained when my father kept us home to work in the field, but she encouraged us to work hard so we could finish and go to school. My brothers were able to put in a few hours before it got dark after they got home from school. I never knew whether they tried to get home early to help us, but I could not blame them if they did not. I would not wish our fate on anyone.

Eventually the cotton was all picked and sent to the gin for processing around late October. Then, my father woulg go to settlement with his boss. He usually grossed around five thousand dollars per season from the sale of the cotton. During that time five thousand dollars was a lot of money for a black man and his family. From the money my father made from the sale of the cotton, his boss subtracted his debts from the total amount and my father got the balance. After his debts were paid, he would net around thirty-five hundred dollars or more.

My father was very unfair to my mother and his family. His fairness was to give my mother one hundred dollars for her and the four children. She used the money to buy us shoes and clothes for school and church. My mother was very grateful for her children who had left home and would send money back to her so she could buy us clothes for school. Sometimes my sister would send us clothes as well. One time my father took the balance of the money from his cotton sale and purchased an old car. He had to push it off the lot, because it was defective. He also used the money to go on drinking binges. He would get drunk and physically abuse my mother and us children for no real reason. I remember this cycle went on for several years.

My father was labeled the town drunk; and the school children would always make fun of us while we were in school or in the neighborhood. Instead of calling me Delores, some students would call me "Ike," which was my father's name. He would get drunk and many times were put in jail for being drunk in public. During those times when he was locked up on the weekends, we would be so happy because we knew we would have peace for at least one night. He usually got locked up on Saturday night and his boss would pick him up on Monday morning when it was time for him to go to work. As the white family's father and mother got older, the sons eventually decided that my father was not of any great value to them anymore. They stopped him from sharecropping and I think they asked him to move from the farm. We moved to a small town called St. Matthews, S.C. By this time, my two brothers and sister had also moved away from home. I was the only one living with my parents. When my eldest sister moved to Washington, D.C., she provided a place for us to come to when we graduated from high school. She was a surrogate mother for all of us. One brother went to the Army and eventually moved to D.C. after he got out of the Army. My other brother and sister moved to D.C. after graduating from high school and I moved there the day of my graduation.

There was brokenness throughout our family. My mother was broken because she worked hard, took care of her children, and was in an abusive relationship. Many times we asked her why she stayed in the marriage with my father, and she always said these words, "I will keep my family together." She endured a lot of pain for that purpose, but she was not deterred. She made a covenant with God and her husband when she got married and to every child she brought into the world. She loved us, taught us, and encouraged us to be the best that we could be. She introduced all of us to God at an early age. She let us know that God's grace kept us. We went to church every Sunday, whether we had transportation or not (most of the time my father's car was not working). We had to walk many miles to get to church. Sometimes we would get a ride and sometimes we had to walk all the way. It was on one of our Sunday morning walks to church when I met my oldest brother. He was in the Army at that time. It was only my mother and me walking that morning for some reason. A car stopped and this handsome man got out of the car. He was dressed in his Army uniform with the hat to match. He came across the road, hugged and kissed my mother, and picked me up and said, "I am your oldest brother!" That was the first time I could remember seeing him.

My mother was determined to make it on broken pieces. God was with her at all times. Sometimes I would hear her calling on the name of Jesus without any apparent reason. She did not allow us to give up on anything that we were doing. I heard that my brother wanted to quit school at one point because of the distractions with my father in the home, but she would not allow it. She made him stay in school and the rest of us did not even think about quitting. After my brother realized he could not quit school, he graduated with honors and the rest of us graduated at the top of our game.

My mother's strength came from God. She had seven children to become productive citizens in society. When my father died she was broken; they had been married for at least forty years. She mourned her loss, but she eventually came around and took control of her life. As seen in the Scripture in Acts 27, God encourages those who suffer for Him to trust in Him. My mother trusted in God; even in her suffering, she knew that God was there for her. She purchased her first home at the age of sixty, and paid for it in full after twelve years. When she died at age eighty-five, she left the home to her children. You can make it on broken pieces!

My siblings and I drew strength from my mother and father. My father's life was painful as well. His mother died when he was a baby, so he grew up without his mother's love. He suffered from low-self esteem. He never learned to read or write, so he used alcohol and his aggressive behavior to make himself feel better. My mother was his saving grace, but he sometimes appeared to despise her because she could read and write. When he was drinking, he would snatch her reading material from her.

He spent a great deal of his life in the church and he wanted to preach the Word of God, but he could not persevere in that arena because of his demons, alcohol and abusive behavior. Eventually he stopped going to church, but he continued to preach around the house when he had his power juice (alcohol). His behavior did not stop him from being a father in the home. He instilled in us the importance of going to school to continue our education. After we finished gathering my father's crop, he did not allow us to miss any more days from school and he did not allow us to work for anyone else, not even the white family he worked for.

Whatever crop needed attending, we had to do it after school. He was also active in our school activities. He let the principal of the school know who his children were and if something was going on in the school, he would make sure to check things out, such as what time activities started and what time they ended. When I went to my senior prom, I did not get home until after 1:00 a.m. in the morning. It was traditional for the seniors to go to a party after the prom. Around noon the next day, my father came home and said, "Mr. Parker (the principal) said the prom was over at 12:00 midnight." He never asked me where I was, but I knew he had made a point of going uptown so he could talk to the principal about the time I got home.

My mother grounded us in the spiritually and sociallly. She had an eighth grade education, but she had the desire to continue her education. She was an avid reader; therefore, we had lots of books around the house to read at will. She received a wealth of knowledge by working with the white families. She was the maid for a mother, father, their three sons, and their wives. She cared for their children and traveled with them on vacation. She taught us how to be comfortable with what God had provided us with and how to humbly follow our dreams. As I stated before, attending church was not an option, it was a priority for us to go church every Sunday. She also taught us how to be productive citizens. She made us keep the house clean, wash clothes, paint, and cook. We kept the yard clean as well! We actually swept the yard with a broom! How clean is that! We were not allowed to drop any trash in the yard or anywhere around the property. My parents rented their house while we were growing up, but we respected our home as if we owned it. My mother would not have it any other way.

I credit my mother with emphasizing the importance of family. She would not allow us to do anything to hurt the other. She charged the oldest to take care of the youngest and when she was away from home, the oldest was in charge. There was never any fighting among us siblings. We never argued with each other. I remember crying to follow my sister when she went to visit with my cousin at my grandparent's house. I would cry and wallow in the dirt, grass, and everything else. Sometimes my mother would make my sister stay home with me and sometimes she would let her go. When she allowed her to go with my cousins, she would talk to me in a loving way to calm me down. After all, I was the "baby" and I wanted to have my way. She also let me know the importance of extended family as well. We would walk about fifteen miles or more to visit our grandparents.

We were taught to respect everyone, including the elders, our aunts, and uncles. We attended family outings and enjoyed happy times with our cousins. My mother made sure we gave equal respect to my father's family. My grandmother on my father's side died when my father was a young child, but I met my paternal grandfather and his second wife. My father had ten sisters and brothers and my mother had five brothers and four sisters; she was the oldest child. As I am writing this book, my mother and seven of her siblings are dead. Her two youngest sisters are still living. My father and nine of his siblings are dead; one sister is still living.

My mother taught me a lot about self-control. She was highly addicted to smoking cigarettes. She never drank alcohol, but she enjoyed smoking. When she did not have money to buy cigarettes, I recall her walking along the highway picking up cigarette butts to smoke. One day she told us that she was not going to smoke anymore, and she stopped "cold turkey." I did not know why she stopped smoking, because I was still very young, but as I look back on those days, she must have found out that smoking was detrimental to her health and she made the decision to stop.

Both of my parents were great people. A few years ago as my husband and I and my brother and his wife were traveling in South Carolina, my sister-in-law said, "Your father used to drink a lot and you all laughed at the things that he said and did while he was drunk, but he was always faithful to his wife and his family. He never had any children outside of the family." I was shocked when she said that because I had never given that a thought. As a matter of fact, I thought that was the norm. It should have been the norm, but since she brought that to my attention, I started looking at family dynamics in my extended families and other families and I realized that was not the norm. Many husbands and wives during that time had children outside of their marriage. My parents made it on broken pieces, but they showed us how to use what we had to make it. As I reflect on my life, I realize that there are many areas in my life that are broken, and many areas that are solid. As in the Scriptures, I will make an assessment to see how I can use the solids to support the brokenness.

Personal Reflections

My humble beginnings could have been a stumbling block for me, but I choose to use the broken pieces to climb across those stumbling blocks and move to higher grounds. As I was growing up, I never knew what was going on in the household of other family members, or my peers' families. However, many of my family members and classmates died early from alcohol and drug abuse. Why is that? Were their lives broken?

My mother was a hardworking domestic worker. She cleaned house for an entire family and their children's family, but unknowingly to them, she brought pieces of a dream home with her every day. We could not afford to buy the daily newspaper or magazines. When her employers gave them to her to put in the trash, she would bring them home. When she brought those amenities home, we took full advantage of them. I read every newspaper and every magazine she brought home. My dreams of interior decorating came from reading those magazines. I also loved reading stories about people who were successful in their endeavors, whether it was winning the spelling bee or starting a successful business.

My strong belief values encouraged me to take steps of faith to accomplish my heart's desires. As we all know *"Faith without works is dead,"* so I always worked hard to accomplish my goals. I took control of my destiny at an early age. I decided that I wanted to achieve higher grades in school, so I worked hard to get them. I decided that I was not going to let my father's embarrassing actions of being locked up for being drunk in public places lower my self-esteem. My peers tried hard to use my father's actions to make jokes in my presence, but I did not cry or hang my head. I did what I could do to motivate myself. I knew at an early age that I was not responsible for my parents' actions. So I did not let those jokes bother me, well not too much anyway. I could always be smarter than those jokesters could, and I made that my goal and was successful. I had one classmate who never called me Delores or Dee; he always called me "Ike," (my father's name). He turned out to be an alcoholic who died before we had our tenth high school reunion. Maybe he admired my father for some reason and followed in his footstep. He probably thought the alcohol gave him courage, something he may have desired. Who knows?

At the end of the day, please know that our life is not perfect, but we can take what we have and make it better. We are to make the best out of every day by forgetting our past and looking to the future. What would you like to do in the future? When your parents brought you into this world alive, you were given a ticket for abundant life. Take every piece that is offered to you and build your life. We are all God's children. When we acknowledge God and recognize that our strength comes from Him, we can do all things.

Reflection

Take a few minutes to reflect on your life and search for some brokenness that may have affected your life negatively. Write them down in the space below:

_____

_____

_____

_____

_____

_____

_____

_____

_____

_____

_____

To everything there is a season, and a time to every purpose under the heaven (Ecclesiastes 3:1).

Chapter 2

Adopt the "Me" Attitude; "Love Yourself"

Hatred stirs up strife, but love covers all sin (Proverbs 10:12).

We must first learn to love ourselves. We need to feel good about ourselves, not deny the need to love ourselves. We will not have the power or strength to move from one challenge to the other unless we love ourselves.

If you have had a life full of self hate, how do you flip the switch to self love? We know that Jesus said in Mark 12:30-31, *"Love the Lord your God with all your heart and with all your soul and with all your mind and strength and Love your neighbor as yourself. There is no commandment greater than these.*" We learn several things from this Scripture: Love God, love yourself, and love your neighbor. Since we know what Jesus said and since we believe and have faith in God's Word, we can start looking at ourselves in a different light. Adopt the "Me" attitude. I love God; I love myself; and I love my neighbor. My body is my temple and I must honor it as I honor God. The Holy Spirit dwells in this temple and my temple should be fit for the King of this temple.

Loving yourself, or self-love, may have the tendency to sound selfish; therefore, some people will have a hard time allowing themselves to love themselves. They look at the term self-love as being someone with an excessive amount of pride or the type of love that shuts everyone else out because they only care about themselves. The Free Dictionary by Farlex defines self love as the instinct or tendency to seek one's own well-being. So you see, you can love yourself and not be selfish. In order to love yourself, you must have self-esteem. If you lack self-esteem, you are not accepting yourself as that unique person God made. If you do not accept the unique person that you are, you are rejecting yourself and your uniqueness.

If you find yourself hating something about yourself, you must accept yourself first and then after accepting or loving yourself, you can change that particular thing that you dislike. For example, most people have problems with their outer appearances, such as hair, eyes, teeth, skin color, size, weight, etc. Well you must learn to love everything about your appearance and then if you have something you want to change, proceed to work on that area. If there is something on your body that you cannot change, you have to learn how to love those things more than any other part of your body and focus on those areas so you can make changes where you can.

Personal Testimony

Here is a personal testimony about a part of my body that I do not love, but cannot change. I am the youngest girl in my family, but I have the larger body frame, so ironically, I have the largest feet. I wear a size eleven shoe and my sisters wear sizes nine and ten respectively. It is always a challenge for me to find shoes in my size, because either the shoe companies do not make a lot of size elevens or the size elevens are the first ones to leave the store shelves. I pay close attention to the types of shoes that I buy. I make sure that my shoes make my feet look slender, so when I find a pair that I am satisfied with, I buy them in all of the colors available. I cannot change my shoe size, but I love myself enough to focus on my feet. If I did not make the effort to work on that area, it could cause low self-esteem for me.

Please know that the most important thing is for YOU to be comfortable with yourself. As far as the shoe story goes, others looking at me may have some negative comments about my shoes, but when I am secure in whom I am or what I like for me, it will be very hard for a negative comment to shake my level of confidence.

There are many other ways you can help yourself become more comfortable with yourself. Enhance your mentality by reading self-help books, listening to motivational tapes, and attending workshops. Attend church services on a regular basis. Join support groups in your church and be productive by working in a ministry that interests you. Re-invent yourself by taking on special projects in a support group or at home. Take classes to enhance your learning.

Therapy is another powerful tool for self-help. When I entered the chaplaincy program, my supervisor urged my peer group members and me to go to therapy. At first, I could not understand why that was so important. My supervisor insisted that therapy would be beneficial to each one of us. At the time, I did not realize that my health benefits covered therapy sessions. (The more you learn, the more you realize what you do not know.) I went on line and found a therapist that was covered by my health care provider; I agreed with my supervisor; that was the best thing I could have done for myself. During my first visits, I shared my life story; I shared problems and issues that I had been dealing with for years and not talking about, because I did not have that safe place or person in which to share. When I shared my story or any concerns, I would leave my therapist's office feeling great and could not wait until the next visit to get back.

During my first visit, I shared with my therapist the trials that I was going through with a very sick brother and a terminally ill sister. Without any pre-planning, I started crying during the session, and did not stop for thirty minutes. The therapist sat quietly and let me cry until I stopped. I felt so much better when I left that day; and I was able to reach out and help other family members.

Personal Testimony

I am always looking for something new and exciting to do. I never turn down an opportunity to learn something new. I moved to Washington, D.C., to live with my older sister as soon as I graduated from high school. Two months later, I found a job working at the local telephone company. (Thanks to my youngest brother who delivered meat for a local meat company.) During his travel, he saw a job advertisement for the local telephone company. He called me from a pay phone and told me to apply. I did and was hired immediately as an operator.

I started college shortly after starting my new job. My tenure in college was short lived, because I wanted to get married and start a family. Along with the marriage came the job, a house, two children, and not much time for anything else. During our children's formative years, I worked at the local telephone company and was promoted to several different positions before I retired in 2006.

While working full time, I ventured into direct sales. I sold Home Décor products and Mary Kay Cosmetics; I was quite successful and then I moved into to the real estate business, listing and selling houses in the State of Maryland. Again, I was quite successful. I thought the real estate industry would be the place where I would spend my time after I retired from the telephone company. However, I sold more real estate when I was working part time, than I did when I tried to work full time in the industry. I purchased two properties during my tenure as a realtor, one in Baltimore partnering with my sister and girlfriend, and one in Oxon Hill, MD. During that time, I had returned to school and earned a bachelor's degree in Management Studies.

I joined forces with two sisters-in-law and started a retail business, selling women clothing and accessories. Our business was very successful. Our shop was always full on Saturdays. We traveled to New York City to purchase our clothing and jewelry. We had lots of fun doing business together.

Eventually I sold both properties and we closed the store. We were all overwhelmed with our regular jobs and the time and energy we had to put into the store. I was called back to the telephone company to work temporarily as a contractor after retirement. I was rehired in 2001 as a full-time employee at Verizon's

Communications Company and was promoted into a management position at the phone company, where I stayed until I retired in 2006.

I enrolled in a Master of Divinity program at Howard University School of Divinity and earned my degree in December 2003. While I worked, I attended a local Bible seminary, earned my doctorate degree in Religious Studies, and went on to earn my Doctor of Philosophy degree in Philosophy of Religion. During my postgraduate work, I also worked at the seminary as a Professor, Dean of Students, and Vice President of Finance.

A naturopathic doctor began teaching Natural Health and Wellness at the seminary where I worked. I enrolled in his class and learned how to heal my body by eating the right foods and eliminating the bad foods. Dairy products were my biggest culprit! My legs used to ache all the time, and I did not know what caused the pain. I asked the professor about those aches and pains and he told me about dairy products causing uric acids to settle in my joints, causing pain. When I removed the dairy products from my diet, the pain went away.

I had a lot of questions for the professor because I wanted to be healthy. His wife saw how excited I was about eating healthy, so she told me about this Christian company in North Carolina teaching on life-style change. This lifestyle change promotes God's people to return to nourishing their bodies with the garden foods God told Adam to consume in Genesis 1:29: *Then God said, "Behold, I have given you every plant yielding seed that is on the surface of all the earth, and every tree which has fruit yielding seed; it shall be food for you* (NASB).

I immediately went on the internet and found out that I could receive the Health Minister's Training and become certified to teach others and myself how to nourish our bodies with garden foods. I drove to Shelby, North Carolina, for the training. My sister accompanied me. We stopped in Colonial Beach Virginia, to pick up a family friend so she would have company while I attended class. What an experience! The training was excellent!

There were approximately 60 students in my class. The top-level managers in the company, including the founder, taught us. We were served three meals per day of healthy foods such as vegetables and grains. We received no meats and very little starches. We also received supplemental drinks such as Barley Max and Carrot Juice. Surprisingly, the meals were very fulfilling and energizing. With my certificate in hand, I drove the 400 hundred miles back to Maryland with lots of energy left over. I started my Lifestyle Change and Consulting business immediately. My greatest reward is being able to recognize the importance of eating healthy and enjoying the healthy foods that I eat. I also feel great about promoting lifestyle change and sharing information with my family and friends. I love myself, and for that reason, I have no problems sharing with others and helping wherever I can.

I entered the Clinical Pastoral Education (CPE) Chaplain's Intern program at the Washington Hospital Center in D.C. I completed my first Unit in the spring of 2008. In the spring of 2010, I entered the Chaplain's Resident program at the Washington Hospital Center, and completed my fifth Unit of CPE in the spring of 2011.

I will continue to explore and pursue opportunities for myself because I have fun while I am learning. Having fun while improving yourself can go a long way when it comes to loving yourself.

As you start anew on this journey of self-love, please remember the following:

- Love yourself.
- Accept yourself unconditionally and make changes where you can, if you care to do so.
- Be motivated to make changes.

Adopt the "Me" attitude; love yourself. Give God thanks everyday for your blessings and use a positive affirmation every day.

Personal Reflection

In my brokenness, I used the pieces I needed to carry me from one step to the other. God was always there with me. Life was not easy, but I moved swiftly and carried the bitter with the sweet. I prayed for strength and guidance every step of the way. God never let me down. He was always there! When I recognized how much God loved me, I knew I could put Him first and love myself. Loving me meant striving to be the best I could be, but I had to work in order to position myself so God could help me. God will help all of us if we ask Him, and be willing to do our part.

When I was a child, I dreamed about the things I wanted and how I wanted my life to be, but as I grew older I realized that I had to work to make my dreams a reality. The Scripture says in James 2:14, *"Faith without works is dead."* Without knowing it, I started my works back in high school. When I entered into the eleventh grade, I desired in my heart to receive an award on class night, so I focused on the requirements. Even though I did not get the award, I was elected as a class officer; and I delivered a speech on class night.

After years of working in the telephone company, direct sales, and as a realtor, I desired to complete my education. When I inquired with human resources (HR), I found out that the company would pay my tuition in full. I was responsible for maintaining a C grade average in each course. I took that opportunity to complete my education. It was not an easy task. I had to take a course in remedial math before I could take the core college courses. I worked hard and completed the remedial course in one semester. I worked diligently to complete an associate degree in Business Management, bachelors degree in Management Studies, and a Masters of Divinity degree, while working at the telephone company. In addition to college degrees, I also took certificate courses to obtain my real estate licenses.

My education helped me to move from one position to another within the company. It also increased my level of confidence. I was confident enough to ask for what I wanted; and most times God would open doors for me to receive what I wanted or needed. God is awesome! He opened doors for me that I could not open myself. In one incident, God showed me favor. I asked my supervisor to allow me to take a computer class to enhance my computer skills. He allowed me to go to the class at the community college during work hours; the company paid for the course and paid me while I took off a week to attend class. I had no idea that I was going to receive that type of grace before I asked. I felt like I could accomplish any task because I knew God would give me the strength and knowledge that I needed then and He continues to give me strength every day. Philippians 4:13 encourages me, so I recommend this Scripture to you: *I can do all things through Christ which strengtheneth me.*

Another major blessing came to me on the job by the hands of God, a blessing that man alone could not have orchestrated. After being on the job for approximately twenty-seven years, I began to prepare for my retirement. In doing so, I began to look at another job title that would take me to the highest paying non-management job in the company. I wanted to move to the marketing and sales line of business to make more money to improve my retirement benefits. I applied for the job, passed the written test, and was called for an interview. The interview was canceled for some reason, so I began to investigate. I could not get any answers so I filed a grievance against the company via the local union. I did not get any satisfaction from the union because they did not have any answers for me.

The marketing and sales line of business had a valid reason for not hiring me; I did not have any experience in that field. I was not qualified for that job because all of my time in the company had been spent in another line of business called operations. They did not want to take a chance on me learning the job after being in another line of business for twenty-seven years, because I had not been in any other position that could help me in the marketing and sales position.

I believe God heard my prayers; He knew the desires of my heart, so He sent me to an HR person to inquire about my application. When I called HR, the sweet angelic voice on the other end of the phone said, "I have another position available for you. Why don't you take that position while you are waiting for the union to respond?" I was reluctant at first and said, "That job only pays eleven dollars more per week than I am making now." She insisted sweetly by saying, "There is an office downstairs where those employees work; would you like to go there and sit with them? I could set the visit up with the office manager." Then I heard a voice from God saying, "Go." I said yes and that was the beginning of a historical landmark for me. I accepted that job and approximately a year later, I got the job I wanted. The fight did not stop there, but my ammunition got stronger; now I had marketing experience and my Bachelor of Science degree (which I completed while I was on the job that the HR person suggested I take). I met with management personnel and the union after I signed my name on a list for a civil suit against the company. After the meeting, I was told to apply for the position again, and I was rewarded the job within months.

When you love yourself, you trust in God and use your confidence to help you move to the next level. God used His angel to get my attention. I listen to God every day. When I pray, I ask Him to lead me and guide me. He has not failed me yet.

I desired with all my heart to attend Howard University School of Divinity (HUSD). I called the school many times to receive their brochures. I carried those brochures in my bag until they got old and soiled, and then I would call back for more. There was a stumbling block that I could not get around. Finances! After working in that desired job for two years, I was promoted into management. The company was not paying for management employees to take non-job related courses. I certainly did not want to take out a student loan, as I was planning to retire. Therefore, I kept my brochures in my bag and retired in 2001. Six months into my retirement, I was called back to the company to work as a contractor in a non-management position. I stayed in that position six months and was rehired as a non-management employee. One day when I was sitting in the break room, I overheard an employee telling another employee, "The company will pay for all degrees, non-job related as well." (Another set-up by God!) I immediately went to my desk and called the Tuition Assistance Plan representatives to verify the information. I was told yes, as long as the school had middle states accreditation. The representative verified the school and the rest is history. I enrolled in HUSD in the fall and graduated two and half years later with a Master of Divinity Degree. The songwriter says and I agree, *"Jesus will work it out....if you let Him...."*

When I retired, I received full cash out option, with health benefits. That was beautiful, as long as I was spending money. However, I realized that my money was leaving really fast, so I went back to work. When I was rehired as non-management, I had to work at least 5 years before I became vested to start my retirement funds, which would have been a blessing, but I had my sights set on returning to a management position.

However, there was one little glitch; I was in school and the company would not pay for non-job related courses for management employees. Without any knowledge of future endeavors with the company, I worked hard to finish before the three years were up. I went to school during the summer and took full loads during the fall and spring semesters. While I was in school, I praised God for the management position. I praised and thanked God for a position that I did not know was going to be vacant. I claimed the victory because I know about the goodness of God. I finished my last class in December, and the company offered an exit package to management employees in December and many of them retired with the package. Doors opened for me ...; I was promoted to management in December. Immediately after returning to management, my service time was bridged. Therefore, instead of having three years, I now had thirty-three years with full retirement again. *My God is an Awesome God... He reigns from heaven above....*

I trust the Lord with my life, so whenever I ask for something that I am not rewarded with immediately, after a moment of grieving, I focus on Proverbs 3:4-6 (TLB):

> *[4]If you want favor with both God and man and a reputation for good judgment and common sense, [5]then trust the Lord completely; don't ever trust yourself. [6]In everything you do, put God first, and He will direct you and crown your efforts with success.*

Reflection

Think about yourself. Are you taking care of yourself? Are you loving you? Make notes of the things you do to show yourself love.

_____

_____

_____

_____

_____

_____

_____

_____

_____

_____

Every good gift and every perfect gift is from above, and cometh down from the Father of lights, with whom is no variables, neither shadow of turning (James 1:17).

You Can Make It on Broken Pieces

CHAPTER 3

Helping Others Is Key

Do not neglect to do good and to share what you have, for such sacrifices are pleasing to God (Hebrews 13:16 ESV).

I shared my passion to explore life with a vengeance with my family and friends. During my years of working and going to school, I followed in my mother's footstep by taking care of my family. My husband and I worked as a team to see that our girls had the best that we could give them. There were daycares, after school care, private schools, dance classes, dance recitals, costumes, school programs, homework, graduations, and college. We shared in their pains and their joys. We worked together to help them become productive citizens. My husband and I assisted each other in taking care of our family, our home, and each other. In addition to taking care of my immediate family, I reached out to help my extended family and friends whenever I could. Then God called me into the ministry.

The call to ministry came early in my life, but I did not recognize the call until my relationship with God was strengthened during my spiritual journey. I thought the call to ministry was only about preaching and teaching. My intuitive spirit helped me to understand that helping others was a call to ministry as well. I am very content helping others — doing what Jesus did in His ministry. As I begin to study the Bible for clarity and understanding, Matthew 25:31-46 made an impact on my life; "my call" was validated.

> [31]*"When the Son of Man comes in His glory, and all the angels with Him, He will sit on His glorious throne.*[32]*All the nations will be gathered before Him, and He will separate the people one from another as a shepherd separates the sheep from the goats.* [33]*He will put the sheep on his right and the goats on his left.* [34]*Then the King will say to those on his right, 'Come, you who are blessed by my Father; take your inheritance, the kingdom prepared for you since the creation of the world.* [35]*For I was hungry and you gave Me something to eat, I was thirsty and you gave Me something to drink, I was a stranger and you invited Me in,*[36]*I needed clothes and you clothed Me, I was*

sick and you looked after Me, I was in prison and you came to visit Me.' ³⁷"Then the righteous will answer Him, 'Lord, when did we see You hungry and feed You, or thirsty and give You something to drink? ³⁸When did we see You a stranger and invite You in, or needing clothes and clothe You? ³⁹When did we see You sick or in prison and go to visit You?'⁴⁰ "The King will reply, 'Truly I tell you, whatever you did for one of the least of these brothers and sisters of Mine, you did for Me.' ⁴¹"Then He will say to those on his left, 'Depart from Me, you who are cursed, into the eternal fire prepared for the devil and his angels. ⁴²For I was hungry and you gave Me nothing to eat, I was thirsty and you gave Me nothing to drink, ⁴³I was a stranger and you did not invite Me in, I needed clothes and you did not clothe Me, I was sick and in prison and you did not look after Me.' ⁴⁴"They also will answer, 'Lord, when did we see You hungry or thirsty or a stranger or needing clothes or sick or in prison, and did not help You?' ⁴⁵"He will reply, 'Truly I tell you, whatever you did not do for one of the least of these, you did not do for Me.' ⁴⁶"Then they will go away to eternal punishment, but the righteous to eternal life" (Matthew 25:31-46 NIV).

In those Scriptures, Jesus called us to serve the hungry, the thirsty, the poor, the sick, and even the prisoners. My attitude of helping others is really about serving God's people.

The call to serve led me to my current position as Pastor of New Life Praise Community, Inc. Our mission in summary is focusing on the whole person. In this ministry, after the teaching and preaching, I give each parishioner the opportunity to speak about their joys and concerns. This is a way of helping others relieve themselves of any burden they may have or an opportunity to talk about the joys in their life, with family and friends.

I share with all of God's people; whether they are family members are not. If my husband did not use his godly wisdom to protect me and his family, my home would probably be bursting at the seams with people that I would like to help. I have had numerous family members and friends stay with us when they met some struggles in life or when they needed a place to stay temporarily while they were waiting for a house to be built or until a job came through. When my daughters graduated from college and started working, they were receiving base salaries, which was not enough for them to rent the expensive houses in our area. I asked God to help me to buy a house large enough to rent rooms to young women who were starting out in life and could not afford high rent. Sometimes later, I got the opportunity to do that. I was able to rent rooms to young women throughout the five years that I owned the house. The house in itself was a challenge. It was a huge house with electric heat and no fireplace. My husband and I renovated the house from bottom to top. It was a labor of love, because it was a gift from God. I rented out the basement and the entire upper level until I decided to sell it. The last two tenants, my daughter and another young woman, purchased their own home when they left the house. I thank God for the opportunity to help others.

My eldest sister adopted a four-year-old girl, whom she came to love when she was her foster parent. As she got older, the girl began to display some real behavior problems. She was disrespectful to my sister and adults in general. She was not working in school. She was always fighting and constantly suspended from school. Before she died, my sister tried to get one of her siblings to take her daughter into their home, but because of the child's behavior problem, no one was willing to take on that responsibility. Also, our age was a contributing factor to not taking her in. We are all in retirement age and did not have the finances to take care of her. We were all highly emotional over our oldest sister's illness and all that she was going through, her treatments, and her pain. To know how much my sister loved her daughter and to see her continue to mistreat our sister during her lowest point in life were very unsettling. We were in pain and the child's behavior did not help us.

As my sister got sicker, by way of a friend, I found a group home for the child in southern Virginia. About one month before my sister died, she was able to place her daughter in the group home. Even though she resides in the group home, she still needs a guardian. I felt my sister's pain, so I asked my husband if I could let my sister know that I would take her in after she dies. I knew my husband's feeling about children at this time in his life, but I had to ask. He never said yes or no to me. He said, "Why didn't you become a social worker?" Knowing that she was dying, my sister was very concerned about her daughter's welfare and who would take care of her. While we were together one day, I told her I would look after her daughter and she did not have to worry about any her longer. She was very grateful and she told me that God would bless me for making that decision. When my sister died, I was still confused about my decision, but God showed me how much He had given me; and He reminded me that He was always with me. I moved forward with the guardianship and my brother and his wife said they would help me take care of her. She is to remain in school at the group home until she graduates from high school.

During the time of my sister's illness, my oldest brother came to see her and broke his neck by falling down the stairs in our other brother's house. He also suffered a stroke and stayed in ICU for two months and a few days. I visited him two or three times a week. Because of the damage in his body, he could not talk, but he knew each of us as we entered the room. His eyes would follow us around the room; he would nod his head when we talked to him. Two days before his wife and children moved him back to a facility in his home state, he had a medical procedure that enabled him to talk. He knew all of us and held a long conversation with us. We (his siblings) wanted his wife to place him in rehabilitation in the city where he stayed in the hospital. However, our wishes were neither regarded nor discussed. His wife took him by plane back to his home state on Thursday. I received a call on the following Sunday morning that he was dead. I was very upset; and I blamed his family for moving him. I wrote a long letter to his wife and daughters and told them how I felt. They responded to me angrily. God moved me to apologize for displaying my anger at that time. I am sure they were in pain as well.

I was grateful to be able to talk with my therapist about my feelings. I was angry about my brother's death. I thought the ultimate reason for his death was his immediate family's decision to move him on a plane to a rehabilitation center approximately five hundred miles away, before he had any rehabilitation treatment in the hospital or in a local rehabilitation center. In discussing the scenario with my therapist, I revealed the conversation between my brother and me the day he started talking. As I was trying to exercise his arms and legs, he told me he was tired. I apologized and said, "I will stop bothering you now." He said, "I know what you are trying to do." He left two days later while I was at work. I talked to him on the phone and told him I would come to South Carolina to see him very soon. My younger brother and his wife who was with him at the hospital before he went to the airport said he was trying to respond to me over the phone, but I could not hear him. I really thought at that time that I would see him again. When he died two days later, I blamed myself for not taking off that day to say goodbye to him. When he told me he was tired that night, in retrospect, I think he was saying goodbye and I did not understand him. So out of anger, I lashed out against his wife and daughters because they made the decision to move him. I was also angry with myself for not being there as he was leaving.

My trust and faith in God comforts me by letting me know that my brother's death was out of our control. God is in control of our lives — the beginning and the end. The relationships between his family and me were broken, but I pray to God for healing and mending in all areas. I prayed to God for forgiveness for my sins of judging others. Repenting and asking for forgiveness are pieces that I used to help me make it in this painful area of my life.

My brother died in October 2010 and my sister died February 2011. They were the last two siblings of my eldest siblings group. My mother died in 2001 and my oldest brother died in 2002. My mother died from a massive stroke; my oldest sister died from cancer; my oldest brother died from complications from cancer; and my older brother died from a stroke and complications from a broken neck. I helped them as much as I could during their illnesses and I thank God for allowing me to be there for them. When deaths bring brokenness in a family, the pieces of memories help you make it another day.

Personal Reflections

Because I strive to follow biblical principles, I go to great lengths to help others. There are many Scriptures in the Bible that tells us we should help others, regardless of their status in life. Without Jesus in my life, I would put my own needs and desires before others, but the Bible teaches me in Philippians 2:4 (TLB), *"Don't just think about your own affairs, but be interested in others too, and in what they are doing."* Helping others make me feel very good about myself.

I learned earlier on in life how miserable you can feel when you neglect to help someone when you have it in your power to do so. When I was in the fifth grade, a friend asked me how to spell a word on a spelling test. I misspelled the word purposely for her. When the spelling test was returned to us in class, I made 100 and she did not. She confronted me later and said, "You misspelled that word and you got it right." I felt miserable! From that day forward, I never gave a person wrong information purposely. I found out that there is no pleasure in lying, because you feel miserable when the truth is revealed.

Our key Scripture, Acts 27:10, reads, *"Sirs,"* he said, *"I believe there is trouble ahead if we go on – shipwreck, loss of cargo, injuries, and danger to our lives"* (NLT). Paul showed his concern for the people on the ship, even though he was a prisoner. He advised them of the danger they would bring upon themselves if they continued to sail in the storm. They did not listen to him, but he was concerned about the well-being of everyone on the ship, including himself.

Helping others is very rewarding for me. Since I spend a lot of time working on projects that turn out to be successful for me, I share with others. I share information with my family and friends and in turn, God rewards me with open doors. I have been blessed by many people that God used to help me. When my sister's teenage daughter was giving her trouble, I shared the information with my supervisor, who in turn referred me to a group home in Virginia. After a few months, she was accepted into the program and my sister died in peace, knowing her daughter was out of the city and in a place where she would be monitored closely. After my sister died, I became her daughter's guardian. My husband and I provide a home for her to come to when she is on break from school.

God blessed me with many friends on the job who supported me. In particular, one friend I met helped me to do a job that was totally out of my area of expertise. She was very knowledgeable about the job and did not mind sharing. I was very grateful for her support. After I was promoted, I encouraged her to apply for a promotion. When she was ready, I reached out and helped her prepare for her promotion. She was very grateful for my help.

Another friend was instrumental in helping me enter the Clinical Pastoral Education (CPE) program at the Washington Hospital Center in Washington, D.C. We graduated from divinity school at the same time. When she told me about the CPE program, I was not too interested because I was not ready to go into another training program, and did not have the money to pay for the course. I promised her I would consider taking the course later. Of course, she did not stop until I applied for the program. The program was costly and very intense. Again, I was in unfamiliar territory. I had been practicing Christianity all my life, and this program was teaching me about interfaith. Interfaith is respecting and loving people from all different faiths.

I completed one unit and worked a few shifts for pay after the session was completed. The work was hard because the shifts were 12-hour night shifts. I received calls all through the night from all over the hospital. Many calls came in on the weekend because the hospital housed a trauma unit. I finally gave up and decided I was not going back. After a short stint as a substitute teacher, by the grace of God, I received a call from my ex-supervisor who needed a fulltime resident chaplain. The resident chaplain worked and completed 600 hours of education during the four units. I was hired, and worked in that position for 18 months, completing four units of CPE. My last day to work was May 31. I had dreams of being free to travel, write, and play. However, on the twelfth of May, my good girl-friend, the same one who encouraged me to take the first CPE unit, called me and said, "There is an opening for a part-time chaplain in my company. Are you interested?" My first inclination was to say no; but again I heard the voice of God saying, "Don't turn down a job." With a small voice, I said, "Sure." I started working on July 6. The job continues to bless me; and my friend is smiling every day. Look at God!

Jesus speaks about helping others in Matthew 5:16: *In the same way, let your light shine before others, so that they may see your good works and give glory to your Father who is in heaven.*

Reflection

Make a list of the things you have done for others "free of charge" within the last month. Write an emotional word next to each deed. Example: I took my mother to the grocery store. Examples of emotional words: happy, sad, annoyed, etc.

_____

_____

_____

_____

_____

_____

_____

_____

_____

_____

_____

Let brotherly love continue (Hebrews 13:1).

Chapter 4

Brokenness Mending

Take some food, you need it to survive (Acts 27:34a).

As a professional chaplain, I serve the sick and their families as well as the staff in the hospital. As a Natural Health Consultant, I serve my family and the people in the community. I conduct workshops and seminars to teach people how to change their lifestyles for optimal health and wellness.

I am often rejected when I share information with others concerning the foods that we eat. Eating healthy is one of the subjects about which I am very concerned. Certain foods that I eat cause reactions in my body immediately. For example, if I eat any dairy products, my joints will start aching right away. I do not have that problem when I take dairy out of my diet. When I share that information with family and friends, they reject it. Rejection used to hurt my feelings, but because I am in relationship with God, I know that rejections are a distraction. The malevolent forces do not want people to hear the truth about abusing their bodies. I continue to pray and ask God to send another vessel to help them hear the message and give them the strength to care for their bodies as He would have them to, and I believe that He will let them hear that person. God will use any vessel He chooses.

In Acts 27:10-11, Paul was chosen to give the people a message: *"Men, I can see that our voyage is going to be disastrous and bring great loss to ship and cargo, and to our own lives also."* *But the centurion, instead of listening to what Paul said, followed the advice of the pilot and of the owner of the ship.* Paul was in communication with God the entire time and then the angel of God appeared before Paul saying, *"Do not be afraid, Paul. You must stand trial before Caesar; and God has graciously given you the lives of all who sail with you"* (Acts 27:24). When Paul received the message from God, he encouraged the men to hold on because everything was going to be all right. He told them that he had faith in God and everything would happen just as God said it would. I am in communication with God at all times. God has opened my eyes to see the danger that certain foods has brought into my life and the lives of my family and friends. I traveled to North Carolina to take a course in natural nutrition so that I could help my family change their diet and lifestyles. Food is nutrition for our body, so therefore we must eat to be healthy. The problem is we have become slaves to food. My naturopathic doctor coined this phrase, "We live to eat, not eat to live." In these Scriptures, Apostle Paul is encouraging the people on the ship to "eat to live:"

> [33]"Just before dawn Paul urged them all to eat. "For the last fourteen days," he said, "you have been in constant suspense and have gone without food – you haven't eaten anything. [34]Now I urge you to take some food. You need it to survive. Not one of you will lose a single hair from his head." [35]After he said this, he took some bread and gave thanks to God in front of them all. Then he broke it and began to eat. [36]They were all encouraged and ate some food themselves. [37]Altogether there were 276 of us on board. [38]When they had eaten as much as they wanted, they lightened the ship by throwing the grain into the sea" (Act 27:33-38).

I made a personal commitment to myself to make the necessary changes in my life to my diet and lifestyle. Approximately five years ago, I met a naturopathic doctor who helped me change my life. At the time, I was on the Standard American Diet known as

"SAD." The Standard American Diet consists of eating anything and everything with no restrictions.

The Doctor performed a test on me using a technical monitoring device. Health practitioners use this to help patients choose the right solution for their bodies at the right time. The test showed that my arteries were clogged. I was shocked! I had been diagnosed by my medical doctor with high cholesterol, but I did not relate the diagnosis with clogged arteries. When I received the results from the naturopathic doctor about the clogged arteries, I got serious because my mother died from a massive stroke at the age of eighty-five, and the doctor told us her arteries were clogged.

I shared my fear about my mother's illness with the naturopathic doctor and he assured me that if I did not change my diet and lifestyle, the same thing would happen to me. That did it for me! I was determined that I would start that same day with the lifestyle change. The first thing I had to do was order the supplements he recommended for me to take and start the diet he outlined for me. I started taking the supplements and dieting at the same time. In less than two weeks, I could see some results in my looks and how I felt. I was amazed at how good I felt after I changed my diet and lifestyle. I immediately shared this information with my entire family and friends, who eventually had the test and joined forces with me in the diet and lifestyle change.

The illnesses we had in my family ranged from high blood pressure, high cholesterol, arthritis, gout, and diabetes to illnesses that have not been diagnosed, but described as pain in the leg, neck, shoulder, stomach, and more. We were all on prescription medicine of some sort to treat our symptoms. Therefore, we had the same symptoms that could be eliminated by changing our diets and life styles.

The staple foods in our household during our formative years were white rice, grits, and breads. The meats were pork (all cuts), chicken, beef, and fish. Pork and chicken were the most common meats because pigs and chickens were raised on the farm and easily accessible. We had lots of dried beans, peas, collard greens, kale, mustard greens, rape greens, rutabagas, string beans, corn, white potatoes, and sweet potatoes, which were also grown on the farm. We were considered healthy children and my parents were healthy as well. So what does that say about our diet? Why are there so many illnesses in our community today?

The aforementioned foods were given the name of "Soul Food" during the 70's and were featured in restaurants all over the United States. Soul Food was known as the foods served exclusively in the black community. It was a great seller in black community restaurants known as "Soul Food Restaurants." Today, we are still eating the same foods with a little variety. I believe the problems with our foods stem from the additives that are added to the plants and vegetables that we purchase today. Also, the demand is so high for meat, poultry, and seafood all over the world that the animals are forced to produce faster. Could it be that hormones are added to their diet to promote faster growth and production and those hormones are passed on to us as consumers?

After I started on my lifestyle change, I started doing research on my own to find out more about foods that I put in my body and how my body is affected by those foods. This book is written to help you make some changes in your life so you can feel better and look better. The "Soul Food" is still the same, but we have to pay close attention to where the foods are grown or manufactured and how the food is cooked. The word "Soul Food" carries the connotation that the food is cooked with lots of butter, cheese, and fat meat. If that is the truth, then we must move away from "Soul Food," and move to a diet change that will help us maintain optimal health and wellness.

In addition to the over consumption of "Soul Food," we are guilty of irresponsibly feeding our bodies with anything that is deemed to be edible or drinkable. We are not supplementing our diet, because we eat until we are stuffed and do not see the need for supplements because the stomach is full. Most people do not realize that they do not get the proper amount of nutrition from their foods for various reasons, including overcooking our foods and adding items to our food that negate the healthy contents. We consume too much sugar and fat, and we do not drink enough water. We are our worst enemies when it comes to how we treat our bodies.

The Bible gives us the perfect diet in Genesis 1:29: *Then God said, "I give you every seed-bearing plant on the face of the whole earth and every tree that has fruit with seed in it. They will be yours for food.* The question becomes, does God want us to be vegetarians? Some say yes according to His Words in Genesis 1:29. Can you eat seed bearing plant and live and be healthy? Yes, you can; however, you must add some nutritional supplements for optimal health. The Bible says in 1 Corinthians 6:19-20, *[19]"Do you not know that your body is a temple of the Holy Spirit, who is in you, whom you have received from God? You are not your own; [20]you were bought at a price. Therefore honor God with your body."* Since we know that our body is a temple of the Holy Spirit, we should take care of our body for the glory of God. When we overload our bodies with foods that are not conducive for optimal health, we are not honoring our God-given temple.

During the course of my research, experience, and testimonies, I have found that there should be more emphasis on the whole person. While in therapy and in my natural health training, I see the importance of focusing on the non-physical aspects of health, the mind, body, and spirit. When I am teaching Health and Wellness at a seminar or in a class, I teach on caring for the whole person. WHO (World Health Organization) defines health as a state of complete, physical, mental, and social well-being and not merely the absence of disease or infirmity. So therefore, we are not healthy unless we have balance in the whole body. When someone is sick, our goal is to promote healing to prevent him or her from getting sick by caring for the whole body. Healing means making whole, so therefore my treatment is focused on making you whole. When I teach at seminars or consult with patients and give them a list of their lifestyle change recommendations, I treat them with an expectation of their healing from within. In order to heal, we must be aware of the whole body. Before we begin to deal with our eating habits and supplements, let us start with the whole person.

The following definitions are found in Free on line dictionary:

Body

The complete material structure or physical form of a human being. Your body is the housing for your mind and spirit. The body includes all aspects of your being.

Mind

The human consciousness that originates in the brain and is manifested especially in thought, perception, emotion, will, memory, and imagination. Your mind is the seat of thought and memory: the center of consciousness that generates thoughts, feelings, ideas, and perceptions, and stores knowledge and memories. Your mind gives you the capacity to think and understand and the ability to concentrate.

Spirit

The vital principle or animating force within living beings. The force that will rouse or inspire somebody to take action or to have strong feelings. A standard of moral or ethical decision-making. The part of a human associated with the mind, will, and feelings.

It makes good sense to tend to the entire body for optimal health! Now that we have reached an agreement that self-love is important to a healthy diet and life style change, we can move on to the next level of importance for optimal health.

If you have attended any of my health seminars, or health and wellness workshops, you know that I teach on the basic foundations for a healthy lifestyle. During my research on natural health and wellness, I found that prevention starts with the basic nutritional principles. In order to prevent sickness and be healthy you must be disciplined. As I pointed out in my introduction to this book, "nothing is new." You have heard this information repeatedly, presented in different formats, at different times, and by different people.

Drink Water Daily!

I prefer to start my patients on their new journey to health and wellness on their first appointment with me. I do not want to spend an hour talking to my patients about their diet, advising them of their needs to get healthy, and sending them out of the office with a piece of paper with a diet in their hand so they can get started next week or never. Sometimes people want to hear your opinion, but they want to take their time to get started on their change process. I keep a case of water in my office so I can give my patients their first bottle of water so they can get started right away. Water is the single most important nutrient for our bodies. The average adult can live no more than five days without water. Water plays a vital role in regulating body temperature, transporting nutrients and oxygen to cells, removing waste, cushioning joints, and protecting organs and tissues.

Personally, I can tell you that drinking the proper amount of water has many benefits. I feel better when I do it. I do not have stiffness in my legs; my back does not hurt when I get up after being seated for a long time; my skin looks vibrant and clear; and the joints in my knees and fingers feel better. Sometimes when I get hungry, I drink water and the hunger goes away. I recommend you do your research on the type of water you drink.

For optimal health, I recommend one-half of your body weight in ounces for your daily intake of water. For example, if your weight is two hundred pounds, you should be drinking one hundred ounces of water per day. That is equivalent to one point five gallons of water per day. (Please consult your medical doctor before you make any drastic change to your diet). I would suggest you start drinking water as soon as your feet hit the floor in the morning. Drinking this amount of water may require many trips to the bathroom per day, so discipline yourself to drink when you have access to the bathroom. You should sip your water throughout the day; drink four to six ounces per hour. Try to complete the majority of your water during the day when you are awake so you can get a good night's sleep.

Personal Testimonies

I woke up one night with a cramp running up and down my left leg. I tossed and turned trying to get relief. The cramp caused my toes to curl up and I could not move them back to their normal position. I asked God to reveal to me a quick fix and immediately the Holy Spirit told me to drink water. I jumped up and drank two eight-ounce glasses of tap water; immediately the cramp went away. I went back to bed and tried to move around to see if the cramp would return, but it did not. As long as I drink water, I am not bothered with cramps.

My seven-year-old granddaughter was complaining to her mother about a pain in her leg, which normally occurred at night. When my daughter told me howher daughter woke up in the middle of the night crying out about the pain she was having in her legs, I asked her how much water she was drinking daily. My daughter was not sure, so I told her to monitor her water intake and make sure she had an ample amount of water per day. As soon as she started drinking water every day, the night pains went away. Now she carries her water bottle to school every day.

Make a decision on the type of water you think is better for you and your family by doing your research. You can find information online, in health books, etc. Be comfortable with your choice.

Follow the rule of drinking one-half of your body weight in ounces per day or at least five to six eight-ounce bottles per day to get started and then progressively work toward your desired goal.

Make this life change a family AFFAIR. Every member in your family will benefit from this lifestyle change. Discipline yourself and get started today. Be a champion for the cause. Take the lead and show your family that you are committed to the lifestyle change. Start today.

Colon Cleansing

The next important step for a healthy lifestyle change is keeping your colon cleaned. This can be done naturally by having healthy bowel movements daily or using some type of therapeutic treatment to assist. Wikipedia, the free encyclopedia, defines colon cleansing (also known as colon therapy) as encompassing a number of alternative medical therapies intended to remove feces and nonspecific toxins from the colon and intestinal tract. Colon cleansing may take the form of colon hydrotherapy (also called a colonic or colonic irrigation) or oral cleansing regimens such as dietary supplements. The rationale for colon cleansing is the concept of "auto-intoxication," the idea that food enters the intestine and rots.

Personal Testimony

When I was a little girl, I could remember my mother asking me if I was having regular bowel movements. At the time, I thought my mother was being very nosey. I considered that a very private act, but my mother thought it was necessary to ask me if I was regular. My mother never explained to me that regular bowel movements were essential for my health. When I grew older, I still did not know that regular bowel movements were essential to my health, but I knew I felt better after I had one. Regular movements for me would be once a week. When I had a bowel movement two or three times a day, I thought I had eaten something to upset my stomach. So much for being healthy! Healthy, timely bowel movements are the first step to detoxification.

I remember going to the doctor when I was about eighteen because I was not having normal bowel movements. The doctor attempted to give me a colon exam by directing me to get on my knees so he could look in my rectum with some type of instrument. I screamed so loud that the doctor refused to examine me any further. I never went back to the doctor again for that exam. Amazingly enough, no one never, ever, told me that I should change my diet or just drink more water. I remember pears would cause me to go to the bathroom two or three times a day. So when I wanted relief, I would eat some pears or take a laxative. Eventually, I resorted to taking laxatives two or three times a month for that once or twice a week bowel movement.

One of my first attempts of trying to take control of my weight was when I joined Weight Watchers. During that time, I learned that I should be having bowel movements at least three times a day. I was shocked! I was informed that the bowel movements should be very natural and not induced by laxatives. I was also informed that drinking water and eating the proper foods would assist me in the process.

Eliminating properly is very important for optimal health. If you do not eliminate properly your body will become a breeding ground for diseases. Your body will also show signs of bacteria "build-up" or toxins in your body. You can see these signs in your skin (pimples and dark spots), in your body (such as large bloating stomach) in a very foul odor when you eliminate, and in bad breath. Your stool will also be very hard and hard to come out. Please remember, backed-up stool is a breeding ground for DISEASE. Do not let your body be a breeding ground for disease!

Personal Testimony

When I am not eliminating properly, pimples sometimes show up on my face, my skin turns to a dark ashen tone, or my breath will have a foul order. As soon I change my eating habit from natural healthy foods to "junk food" my body immediately reacts. My elimination process changes and I feel sick and my body feels very heavy. So please remember to pay close attention to your body's normal eliminating process. If you are not eliminating at least once a day, you should start monitoring your daily solid intake and liquid intake. To help that elimination process, add more fiber, fresh fruits, and vegetables to your diet.

If your diet consists of an ample amount of water, fiber, fresh fruits, and vegetables, you will eliminate properly. If not, see your doctor.

Get started today. Eat an apple every morning while you are drinking your water. Also eat raw celery during the day. This will help you eliminate daily.

Your diet is very important. Changing it is probably the most challenging part of the lifestyle change. My goal is to help you transition as smoothly as possible. During this transition, it is important that you prepare yourself mentally for the challenge. Be sure to impress upon yourself that the changes you make is to confirm the love you have for YOURSELF!

Personal Testimony

I am a recovering fried food junkie. I love fried chicken, fried fish, fried pork chops, and fried steak; anything fried, I love it. Fried chicken was my favorite food. I ate fried chicken at home, from the fast food joint, or at church functions. If the church group planned a dinner and did not have fried chicken on the menu, I would go out and buy a bucket of chicken just so I could get a piece. Whenever our extended family planned a dinner during the holidays, I would make sure fried chicken was on the menu. Now, I have eliminated chicken from my diet, but I still eat fried seafood occasionally, which I am trying to eliminate as well. I believe that we can eat fried food in moderation, but we must be responsible enough to do the research. Find out the source of the food, what type of oil the food is being cooked in, and how much preservative is in the food before you cook it or buy it.

So how easy was it for me to transition to a new lifestyle? Not easy at all. First of all, I had to immerse myself into natural health and wellness training classes so I could actually hear the negative effect that certain foods had on my health. Monitor your food intake carefully. Invest in a nutrition class or course to help you better understand what you should and should not put in your body for optimal health.

Healthy eating is about feeling great, having more energy, and keeping yourself as healthy as possible. You can do this by learning some nutrition basics and using them in a way that works for you.

Your food choices can reduce your risk of illnesses such as heart disease, cancer, and diabetes, as well as defend against depression. Additionally, learning the habits of healthy eating can improve your health by boosting your energy, sharpening your memory, and stabilizing your mood. Expand your range of healthy food choices and learn how to plan ahead to create and maintain a satisfying, healthy diet.

Personal Reflection

When I embarked on the new process of changing my diet and lifestyle, I had to make some drastic changes. First, I stopped eating meat, poultry, and fish "cold turkey." Now I am not sure that was the best way to change my diet and lifestyle, but it did work for me. I dropped about twenty pounds immediately. Also, when I tried to go back to eating meats, my body would reject it. Sometimes I felt like vomiting or I would feel the meat in my stomach for long periods of time. I felt a sense of fullness sometimes for two days. Then I started looking at a simpler and satisfying way to satisfy my appetite. I wanted to be successful and satisfied with my lifestyle changes. I started managing what I ate and searching out new recipes so the foods that I ate would be tasty and filling.

In addition to our diet, we must consider some other important aspects for a healthy lifestyle.

Supplements

Our diet is the best place to get the nutrients we need for our bodies, but it is impossible to get enough nutrients from the foods we eat daily. Therefore supplements are the next best things for us. Supplements are very important for your diet. Research has shown that our bodies do not get all of the nutrients we need from the foods we eat. It may be possible to get the proper nutrition if we could grow all of our fruits, vegetables, nuts, meats, grains, etc., but since we cannot, we must use supplements to add nutrition to our diet. Check with your medical doctor or a natural health specialist for information about specific supplements. You can also do the research yourself.

Exercise

Exercise is another key component for a healthy life-style. It does not have to be something that you loathe. Make your exercise fit your schedule. I find that a really good exercise for me is jumping on a trampoline. When I get up in the morning, immediately after meditating and reading, I get on the trampoline and jump for about fifteen minutes before taking my shower. If I do not feel like going downstairs to the exercise room, I will jump in the bathroom or go into my office and get on the stationary bike for fifteen minutes. Exercise is key for maintaining a healthy life style.

Resting

Resting is very important in maintaining a healthy life-style. According to research, it is recommended that persons should have at least eight or nine hours of sleep per night. Some people may require more or less, but your body will react when you do not get enough rest. Sleep deprivation could cause illnesses in the body.

I require only seven hours of sleep, but my light goes out at 11:00 p.m. whether I want it to go out or not. When the clock strikes 11:00 p.m., I have to be in bed or very close to the bed or I will go to sleep where I am. At 5:30 or 6:00 a.m. in the morning, I wake up automatically. Even if I do not get to sleep by 11:00 p.m. at night, I still wake up at 5:30 or 6:00 a.m. So in order for my day to be productive, I have to make sure I get to bed on time.

The pieces that I have mentioned in this chapter about your health are very important, especially when it comes to moving forward positively. Each piece is dependent on the other. If your body is sick, you will be distracted and may not be able to think positively. Apostle Paul encouraged the people on the ship to eat for he knew what was ahead them. The fierceness of the storm was going to force them to exit the ship before docking, but with God's help and preparation, they could make it.

We must prepare ourselves for success. God will give you what you need to move forward, but you must prepare yourself for what you want.

This leads me to my final chapter. With all of our wisdom, knowledge, and understanding, we would be nothing without God, the source of our every being.

Reflection

List some of the ways you can mend your brokenness. Can you make physical changes or change the way you think about your brokenness?

_____

_____

_____

_____

_____

_____

_____

_____

_____

_____

And the Lord make you to increase and abound in love one toward another, and toward all men, even as we do toward you (1 Thessalonians 3:12).

Chapter 5

The Source of Your Pieces

For there stood by me this night the angel of God, whose I am and whom I serve (Acts 27:23).

God our Creator is the source of all things. He created man in His image with limited knowledge. God wants us to communicate with Him. He wants us to recognize that He is the source of power for each one of us. God gives us free will to make decisions for our lives. However, when we make decisions without asking Him to help us, we make mistakes, and we have to suffer the consequences. Nevertheless, God's mercy endures forever. Acts 27:16-20 says, *¹⁶And running under a certain island which is called Clauda, we had much*

work to come by the boat: ¹⁷*Which when they had taken up,*
they used helps, undergirding the ship; and, fearing lest
they should fall into the quicksands, strake sail, and so were
driven. ¹⁸*And we being exceedingly tossed with a tempest,*
the next day they lightened the ship; ¹⁹*And the third day we*
cast out with our own hands the tackling of the ship. ²⁰*And*
when neither sun nor stars in many days appeared, and no
small tempest lay on us, all hope that we should be saved was
then taken away. The people used their own knowledge
and abilities to navigate the ship. There was no communication with God from the people in charge. They
were using their intellect to help them move through
the storm.

When we are going through storms in our lives, we
sometimes forget to call on God because we think there
is no way out. Like the people on the ship, we floun-
der in darkness. We forget about God, who can do all
things--our awesome God, who performs miracles after miracles in our lives. Like the people on the ship,
without God you will give up all hope. Everything is
so gloomy until you cannot see any way out of your
situation. I encourage you to look to God for your help
in all things.

Personal Testimony

Early on in our marriage, before our daughters started
school, I wanted to move to a different neighborhood
with better schools. I did not ask God for guidance nor

did I pray to Him for help. We were already struggling with a mortgage, car note, and babysitter fees in addition to our daily living expenses. My husband challenged me by saying we could move if I got a promotion and brought more money home. I got the promotion and we proceeded to look for a new house. We decided we were not going to exceed fifty thousand dollars for the cost of the house. We were selling our current house for thirty thousand dollar, so we were going to use the proceeds from our current house to purchase the second house, but we wanted an affordable mortgage. When we looked at the houses in other neighborhoods in the fifty thousand dollar range, we were not getting more room in that price range, so of course we had to move up to the sixty thousand plus range.

We found our home and I was happy. My happiness did not last for long, because we encountered one problem after the next. We could not put the children in public school because of the school hours. With both parents working, we needed before and after care. The real problem for me commenced with before and after care, when the daycare provider could not see my oldest daughter (she was five at the time) to the bus, because she was sitting for other children. I felt safer placing her in private school and my baby girl was at the daycare all day.

Then there was a problem with our transportation. My new job was in Virginia and my husband worked in

D.C. We were going in different directions so we could not ride to work together. We could not afford two new cars, so we took turns driving old cars to work. I remember driving a Volkswagen with faulty brakes to work. For a while, my husband drove a Mustang with no windows or heat. Someone was praying for us because I did not have a personal relationship with Jesus Christ and I was not asking for directions. I was just moving, putting out one fire after another. I worked overtime and my husband worked a second job to make ends meet. One Christmas our girls were hurt and disappointed, because we could not buy them a particular gift. It seems all of their friends got the gift. We were as hurt as they were but we just could not afford it.

My husband and I were both under a lot of stress as we were trying to balance our lives. We blamed each other for the pressures of life; therefore, our marriage suffered. We were not happy in our marriage, but we could not see any way out of our situation. We had the jobs, the children with private schools and daycare, dance classes, costumes, the mortgage, and car notes.

I was introduced to a direct sales business selling Home Décor products, which I successfully sold for a few years. On my day job, I was moved in to a position that had a lot of overtime. As I worked overtime, my husband took care of the children; after work, he picked them up from school, fixed dinner, and helped with homework. Eventually things got better.

Then I became ill with hyperactive thyroid condition. I was very sick before my illness was diagnosed. It was during that time that I began to seek a relationship with God for myself. I did not have anywhere else to turn. I had two young girls in school, my husband and I had shared responsibilities, and I needed to be able to work to take care of my share. I began to pray to God to help my family and me. God answered my prayers and our lives began to change. My husband and I were able to enjoy some of the pleasures of life and focus on the lives of our growing daughters. I realized that God had not been making decisions for me; He gave me free will and I was force fitting my desires without consulting Him. Even through the storm God was there for my family. He never left us; instead, He showed us how to hold on to Him.

God is so merciful that He will allow the prayers of the righteous to cover many, even if the others refuse to ask His blessings for whatever reason:

> [21] *"Then after long abstinence Paul stood forth in the midst of them, and said Sirs,, you should have hearkened unto me, and not have loosed from Crete, and to have gain this harm and loss.* [22] *And now I exhort you to be of good cheer, for there shall be no loss of any man's life among you, but of the ship.* [23] *For there stood by me this night the angel of God, whose I am, and whom I serve;* [24] *"Saying, Fear not Paul; thou must be brought before Caesar; and, lo, God hath*

*given thee all them that sail with thee." *[25]*Wherefore, sirs, be of good cheer, for I believe God that it shall be even as it was told me. Howbeit, we must be cast upon a certain island"* (Acts 27:21-25).

Even though the people on the ship—the centurion, the master, the owner and prisoners—were not praying to God, Apostle Paul was fasting and praying, and God answered his prayers. The lives of everyone in Apostle Paul's presence were spared because of his faithfulness. He proclaimed to the entire crew that he belonged to God and served Him. God wants us to recognize Him at all times and in all things. He is the source of all goodness.

Personal Reflection

Where do we go from here? I am convinced without a shadow of doubt that God is the source of my strength. Are you convinced that He is everything to you?

In this book, I shared the Scriptures found in the twenty-seventh Chapter of Acts and used comparisons to situations in my life, giving you an inside look at my life, my trials, and my tribulations. There are many stories I could share; but ultimately, you have to look at your life and see God for yourself. God's presence is always with you. He is waiting for you to ask for His guidance and protection. Life is hard, but our God is merciful and good. He will take your broken pieces and make them whole.

I pray that you to take the time to get to know God. He loves you, regardless of your situation. He is always in your presence; just reach out to Him. God's love will give you joy and peace.

Brokenness is temporary; God's love is for eternity.

Reflection

Write a summary paragraph to talk about your source.
Write your testimony concerning your source.

_____

_____

_____

_____

_____

_____

_____

_____

_____

_____

_____

¹In the beginning was the Word, and the Word was with God, and the Word was God. ²The same was in the beginning with God. ³All things were made by him, and without him was not anything made that was made (John 1:1-3).

Conclusion

I am convinced that life is a work in progress. It is a journey that will not be completed until we stop living. We do not know from one day to the next what could transpire in our lives that may change our course of life. Like Apostle Paul, we have to stand tall and say, "I am a child of God! I will forever serve Him!" In Acts 27:31, Paul said to the centurion and to the soldiers, *"Except these abide in the ship, ye cannot be saved."* The shipmen were ready to flee from the ship, but Apostle Paul stopped them; they were setting themselves up to lose their lives. We have to learn to stay with God. Because Apostle Paul was on the ship in constant communication with God, lives were saved.

If you ever feel lost, feel darkness all around you, do not know where to go, and you have lost all hope, read Acts Chapter 27 and look at Apostle Paul's plight. He was a prisoner to man, but he was a child of God. God used him to save himself and the very people that held him captive:

42"And the soldiers counsel was to kill the prisoners, lest any of them should swim out, and escape. 43But the Centurion, willing to save Paul, kept them from their purpose; and commanded that they which could swim should cast themselves first into the sea, and get to the land: 44And the rest, some on boards, and some on broken pieces of the ship. And it came to pass that they escaped all safe to land (Acts 27:42-44).

We allow ourselves to be held captive in life, sometimes by people, circumstances, situations, material things, or emotions. The personal testimonies I shared with you were some areas of brokenness in my life. In each situation, I used pieces to move me to another level. The challenges were hard and sometimes overwhelming, but God carried me when I could not carry myself or when I did not know I needed Him to carry me. I challenge you to encourage yourself to hold on to those positive influences (pieces) in your life and press forward. Stay in the presence of God. He is there for you. With God, each broken piece will move you closer to your destination of love for God, joy in your spirit, and peace forever.

YOU CAN MAKE IT ON BROKEN PIECES!

Scriptures Referencing God as Our Source

Isaiah 40:28-31 - *²⁸Have you not known? Have you not heard? The everlasting God, the LORD, The Creator of the ends of the earth, Neither faints nor is weary. His understanding is unsearchable. ²⁹He gives power to the weak, And to those who have no might He increases strength. ³⁰Even the youths shall faint and be weary, and the young men shall utterly fall, ³¹But those who wait on the LORD Shall renew their strength; They shall mount up with wings like eagles, They shall run and not be weary, They shall walk and not faint.*

Isaiah 58:11 - *The LORD will guide you continually, and satisfy your soul in drought, And strengthen your bones; You shall be like a watered garden, And like a spring of water, whose waters do not fail.*

Jeremiah 17:5-8 - *⁵Thus says the LORD: "Cursed is the man who trusts in man And makes flesh his strength, Whose heart departs from the LORD. ⁶For he shall be like a shrub in the desert, And shall not see when good comes, But shall inhabit the parched places in the wilderness, In a salt land which is not inhabited. ⁷Blessed is the man who trusts in the LORD, and whose hope is the LORD. ⁸For he shall be like a tree planted by the waters, Which spreads out its roots by the river, And will not fear when heat comes; But its leaf will be green, And will not be anxious in the year of drought, Nor will cease from yielding fruit.*

Psalm 84:11 - *For the LORD God is a sun and shield; The LORD will give grace and glory; No good thing will He withhold from those who walk uprightly.*

Psalm 37:1-9 - *[1]Do not fret because of evildoers, nor be envious of the workers of iniquity. [2]For they shall soon be cut down like the grass, and wither as the green herb. [3]Trust in the LORD, and do good; dwell in the land, and feed on His faithfulness. [4]Delight yourself also in the LORD, And He shall give you the desires of your heart. [5]Commit your way to the LORD, Trust also in Him, [6]And He shall bring it to pass. He shall bring forth your righteousness as the light, And your justice as the noonday. [7]Rest in the LORD, and wait patiently for Him; do not fret because of him who prospers in his way, Because of the man who brings wicked schemes to pass. [8]Cease from anger, and forsake wrath; do not fret — it only causes harm. [9]For evildoers shall be cut off; But those who wait on the LORD, They shall inherit the earth.*

Matthew 6:31-33 – *[31]"Therefore do not worry, saying, 'What shall we eat?' or 'What shall we drink?' or 'What shall we wear?' [32]For after all these things the Gentiles seek. For your heavenly Father knows that you need all these things. [33]But seek first the kingdom of God and His righteousness; and all these things shall be added to you.*

Deuteronomy 31:8 - *And the LORD, He is the One who goes before you. He will be with you, He will not leave you nor forsake you; do not fear nor be dismayed."*

2 Corinthians 4:16-18 - *[16]Therefore we do not lose heart. Even though our outward man is perishing, yet the inward man is being renewed day by day. [17]For our light affliction, which is but for a moment, is working for us a far more exceeding and eternal weight of glory, [18]while we do not look at the things which are seen, but at the things which are not seen. For the things which are seen are temporary, but the things which are not seen are eternal.*

John 15:5-7 - *[5]"I am the vine, you are the branches. He who abides in Me, and I in him, bears much fruit; for without Me you can do nothing. [6]If anyone does not abide in Me, he is cast out as a branch and is withered; and they gather them and throw them into the fire, and they are burned. [7]If you abide in Me, and My words abide in you, you will ask what you desire, and it shall be done for you.*

1 Corinthians 2:9-10 - *[9]But as it is written: "Eye has not seen, nor ear heard, Nor have entered into the heart of man the things which God has prepared for those who love Him. [10]But God has revealed them to us through His Spirit. For the Spirit searches all things, yes, the deep things of God.*

1 Corinthians 2:12 - *Now we have received, not the spirit of the world, but the Spirit who is from God, that we might know the things that have been freely given to us by God.*

1 Peter 5:6-7 - *[6]Therefore humble yourselves under the mighty hand of God, that He may exalt you in due time. [7]Casting all your care upon Him, for He cares for you.*

Conclusion

Genesis 22:14 - *And Abraham called the name of the place, The-LORD-Will-Provide; as it is said to this day, "In the Mount of the LORD it shall be provided.*

Philippians 4:19 - *And my God shall supply all your need according to His riches in glory by Christ Jesus.*

James 1:17 - *Every good gift and every perfect gift is from above, and comes down from the Father of lights, with whom there is no variation or shadow of turning.*

(All Scriptures rerefencing God as our source are from the NKJV Bible.)

Delores R. Garvin is a native of Calhoun County, South Carolina. She is the daughter of the late Isaac and Annie Bell Randolph, and the youngest of seven siblings. She grew up in the beautiful hills of St. Matthews, S. C, where she received her primary and secondary education, graduating from John Ford High School. She joined her sisters and brothers in Washington, D.C., immediately after high school and entered Federal City College.

She graduated with a Bachelor of Science degree in Management Studies from the University of Maryland; a Master's of Divinity degree from Howard University School of Divinity, and a Philosophy of Religious Studies degree from Breakthrough Bible College and Seminary in Temple Hills, MD.

Delores' passion for natural health and wellness prompted her to become a certified Health Minister with a commitment to train men, women, and children to obtain optimal health naturally through nutritional support and supplements.

She is currently the pastor at New Life Praise Community Church, in Camp Springs, MD, and she serves as a chaplain in Prince Georges County, providing spiritual care to the sick and their families.

She is blessed to have a loving and supportive family. Her husband Abraham works with her in the ministry, spreading the gospel of the Lord Jesus Christ. They are proud parents of two daughters, Khristahl (Elementary School Teacher) and Adria (Registered Nurse), who reside in the Washington Metropolitan area. Khristahl and her husband Keith Beckett have two beautiful daughters, Keirrah and Kennedi, the grandparents' sweethearts. Delores is also the legal guardian of her endearing niece, Rachelle Davis-Crawford.

Above all things, she gives glory and honor to her Lord and Savior, Jesus Christ! Praise Be To God!

To inquire about book signings or having Delores Garvin speak or minister at your event, please contact:

dgarvin2@verizon.net

or

Dr. Delores Garvin
P.O. Box 441854
Fort Washington, MD 20749

CPSIA information can be obtained at www.ICGtesting.com
Printed in the USA
BVOW030553290812

298897BV00004B/1/P